A RENEWED LIFE:
Life After Death

Janice Clark

authorHOUSE

AuthorHouse™
1663 Liberty Drive
Bloomington, IN 47403
www.authorhouse.com
Phone: 833-262-8899

Published by AuthorHouse   01/25/2021

ISBN: 978-1-6655-1466-8 (sc)
ISBN: 978-1-6655-1464-4 (hc)
ISBN: 978-1-6655-1465-1 (e)

Library of Congress Control Number: 2021901300

Print information available on the last page.

Unless otherwise noted, all scriptures are from the King James Version (KJV)

THE HOLY BIBLE, NEW INTERNATIONAL VERSION®, NIV® Copyright © 1973, 1978, 1984, 2011 by Biblica, Inc.® Used by permission. All rights reserved worldwide.

Scripture quotations marked NLT are taken from the Holy Bible, New Living Translation, copyright © 1996, 2004, 2015 by Tyndale House Foundation. Used by permission of Tyndale House Publishers, Inc., Carol Stream, Illinois 60188. All rights reserved.

This book is printed on acid-free paper.

Contents

Acknowledgement

I would like to thank God for inspiring me to write. Also, thank you family and friends who inspired me to finish what I started. A special thanks to Tamala Richardson for her editorial expertise and Patricia Bohannon for her artistic inspiration.

I love you all deeply.

Introduction

A Renewed Life: Life After Death is what I refer to as a legacy book. A book looking at life after a death. The intent is to provide inspiration, hope and an opportunity to choose life. This book, unites, empowers, and inspires believers to embrace the rights they have as children of God. Their legacy hinges on uniting women....to live according to inspired teachings of His Word. I believe believers need to embrace the inheritance that comes with being sons and daughters of God.

Where does your thoughts go after reading the title, *"A Renewed Life: Life After Death"*? Perhaps you think, how can I go on after a love one has transitioned. Possibly thoughts and feelings of emptiness, void, denial, and the mere absence thereof. Each of these varying thoughts have vivid references to the book, *A Renewed Life: Life After Death*. However, this book does not address the physical death of mankind, but the physical death of

Jesus and the death of the flesh. Flesh, according to Roman 8:7-8 (NLT) is a mind hostile and not pleasing to God. Since we are not addressing physical death, how does a person die and be alive? We put to death our old ways that are in opposition to God (the sinful nature) (Roman 8:13 NIV) "For if you live according to the flesh (old ways), you will die but, if you live by the Spirit you put to death the misdeeds of the body, and you will live."

What does it take to die to your flesh and live by the spirit? You no longer allow your own standards to govern your life, in contrast it is Christ who lives in you that guides your every move. Paul states, "The life he now lives in the flesh is lived by faith in the Son of God, who loved us enough and gave himself for us. The old self has been crucified with Christ (Galatians 2:20 NLT).

Jesus death and resurrection from the cross eradicated the curse of sin for all of mankind. Our responsibility is to safeguard our salvation, renew our minds and you must believe and receive what Jesus has done was complete and you receive Him as Lord over your life. When we accept that truth and His salvation, we can no longer live a sinful lifestyle.

This book is full of lessons and example which shows the importance of how to live after the death of Jesus and how to live a life of faith united with God, His Word and promises during and throughout the transformation.

"Life After Death"

Though our lives have been shaped according to cultural experiences, rearing's, mistakes, exposures, education and more, all have helped fashioned our way of living. These living experiences have molded the minds, behaviors, decisions, characters, habits, and belief systems to respond to others in a fashion not all pleasing to God.

Yet, there is a greater life, the abundant life. The abundant life is the unification of spirit, soul and body and the cultivation of thankfulness for what Jesus has already done, being fully supplied with the fruits of the spirit: love, joy, peace, patience, kindness, goodness, faithfulness, gentleness, self-control of which there is no law (Galatians 5:22-23). These gifts are given freely; therefore, freely give to others.

Life After Death is a daily discovery of this abundant life. Through renewing of the mind, adapting to change, and aligning the soul with God's ways are indeterminable. Regardless of the age and time you accept Him, there will be adjustments, readjustments, alignments, realignments, a continuous renewing of the mind, pruning the things that are not of God and holding fast to the things that are of God. While living a life according to biased values, and standards, those standards become the norm. Now the norms and values that have governed your life may not be the norms that Jesus requires. God norms are founded upon love. Whereas other norms can be a combination of social norms, laws, taboos and more. Norms influence behaviors to conform to its ways and values. Some norms can be so engraved that it resembles you before Christ.

Rhetoric norms must be filtered with regards to the hearts of humankind. Certain norms affect decisions, characters, integrity, lifestyles, behaviors, responses, and shape lives generationally. Change is inevitable but how we respond is optional.

What is living? I believe living is more than being alive. I believe it is a response to the adaptations around you, while learning, growing, developing, and synthesizing. Knowing you have the freedom to be living proof of quality existence. The exact living image of Him, a copy or blueprint likeness of Him with all the benefits to ensure a victorious life.

Living is God's Will. It is important to note the mere fact that you are alive shows the great lengths in which God took to bring you into existence here on Earth. Remember Jesus was born through Mary, where she nurtured Him until maturity. Then He began carrying out His assignment. The process is no different for you or me. We both came through a woman. Let us pause her for a moment and note, it is not as important who your parents are; yet, identifying what is the assignment and purpose of ones being. It is a natural process to want to know where you come from, but do not occupy your thoughts too long there, because far too often we focus on what is not rather than what is. Self-sabotage is spending much of our lives struggling with dysfunctional belief, families, and relationships that are painful. The accumulation of that leads to questioning your identity, capabilities, and assignments. Do not get so caught up in the emotional hype around yourself that you lose sight, fail to discover, and cultivate the gifts within. I hear you, someone asked, what gifts do I have? One might believe he or she is not specifically good at anything. I am inclined to believe differently. It is my belief that everyone has innate talents and unique skills. Throughout my educational career, I have discovered types of skills: hard and soft skills. Hard skills can be easily demonstrated such as, triathlete, pianist, artist, vocalist. Things that come easy for me to do with simple illustrations and demonstrations. Soft skills are skills you cannot see, such as trustworthy, honest, a good listener. There are places where these skills are needed and necessary. Stop and assess yourself. What do you know to be true about yourself? Most likely, you will describe personality traits of which are soft traits. For example, if people would say to you often, you are kind, that is a personality trait (soft trait). Now soft trait skills within itself is not enough to build a career. There are certain skills you are wired with and can improve without changing your personality. For example, having skills in speed, power, agility, reaction time, balance and hand and eye coordination can be used in athleticism. Yet, having the combination of a healthy personality and strong skill set helps in marketing one's abilities. Owning the hard and soft abilities can propel into a potential career or an opportunity to earn money. For example, Are you good at basketball? Sewing? Public speaking? What is the soft skill behind these hard skills? Analyzing, reading and anticipation, articulation, problem solving are some soft skills required by players, speakers, seamstress.

The skills, gifts and talents are given; all comes from God. It is all part of one's DNA. Perhaps the gifts lie dormant, or undeveloped until an appropriate time, if named and received. It is important to access what is willed to us and seized the opportunities as they arrive for the glory of God.

"Reading of the Will"

A type of Reading the Will is a highly anticipated gathering of the family and beneficiaries with the executor and lawyer to hear the members grasp with shock, exclaim in surprise, or eagerly glares at one another. That described reading of the will is mostly seen in movies and Tv show. Realistically, people do not gather in one place for reading of wills, that does not exist in life. In today's world where families are not geographically close, lawyers are required to notify all beneficiaries and provide a written copy of all the beneficiaries and a signature of the document received. In some cases, the executor presents the will to a judge for validity.

Nevertheless, reading of God's Will with family prepares you for spiritual development to withstand the pressures of the world. Reading in groups of like-minded people lends itself to insightful interpretation. Independently reading the will is a form of worship and intimacy. The simplicity of reading the Bible and accepting the things God has already done is His Will. There are other factors which rest on being obedient to the Word of God. The bible is filled with promises, examples, strategies, solutions, and answers to whatever you may encounter in the present and future. Beneficiaries must also have faith to access the promises and become doers of the Word daily.

A good man leaves an inheritance to his children (Proverbs 13:22). Jesus left an inheritance to all His children. Who are His children? In the spiritual Will, sons and daughters who have been born again through the atonement of Christ are the beneficiaries of the WILL. The spiritual process of setting the affairs in order was when God sent Jesus to pay the ransom for all humankind sin. When Jesus died on the cross, He defeated death and rose with all power in heaven and on the earth and declared it is finished. Those who believe now have a right to His inheritance. Without the death of Jesus there will not be an inheritance. Now anyone who believes and receive Him can be delivered from the spiritual death passed from Adam to live again in Jesus.

Upon receiving Jesus as Lord, you will spend the rest of your lives fulfilling, developing, and transforming into the ways, thoughts, actions, behaviors, character, and likeness of Christ. This is a lifelong process to an everlasting abundant life.

There was a writing of the will. This portion is recorded as the Lord was speaking directly to your hearts.

"Belove, My Will contains many Bible promises waiting to be claimed in faith. Be encouraged and know that I your God has your best interest at heart. I sent the comforter of the Holy Ghost to lead, teach and guide you into all truth.

Before you accepted me as Lord and Savior into your life, you were viewed as a sinner. My death settled all sin issues from your past, present and future sins. Therefore, you are no longer a sinner and do not respond or address yourself as such. I the Lord have declared you Righteous!"

Listen to what God is saying to us. "Now learn of me and my righteousness." God is saying, "righteousness is placing you in right standing with "Me your God". Your righteousness will produce righteous actions, righteous behaviors, righteous habits, thoughts, and character all from the Father's righteous values. Righteousness is a gift to whosoever will accept Him by faith (Roman 5:17-18).

This can only happen by grace through faith. You must believe that you are Righteous (good with Him). By grace through faith, you must receive what Jesus has already done on your behalf.

As a child, your parents assured you in the ways of, respect, honor, confidence and cultivated the family's relational values. As a child once you believed what your parents said was taught you began to live and repeat the same truths. Just as you accepted your parent's values when you become believers, you must embrace God's values and seek to learn those values by reading His word and then putting those teachings into practice. Now you must renew your mind into righteous living. Righteous living is the opposite of the world's way or your old way of living. For example, when you experience pain, you will most likely respond by saying what hurts. Righteous living says what God says about pain, which is healing, being healed without doubting. Saying what you see is not faith, it is stating the obvious.

God speaks: "Take my words to heart, because it is through your heart, I see you, not your behaviors. What is in your heart you will speak?"

In righteousness, you say what you see in the spirit of God's Word and what you expect to see fully manifested. Saying God's word in faith until it becomes visual and you can see what you say. By doing this, the spirit is the manifestation of God's promised words. This is what He meant in the scriptures by calling those things that be not as though they were (Romans 4:17). God's word is the guide to "righteous living".

God says to love your enemy, it is the right thing to do (Matthew 5: 44). The natural response to others hurting you is not to love them back; yet, to hurt them as they have hurt you. A renewed mind will be assured in faith that God is the avenger, and He will take care of you. This type of action requires faith building confidence, trust, consistency, studying, reading the word repeatedly. Renewing of the mind is a lifetime journey and process.

God is saying, *I need you to trust me even when you are not sure of the outcome. Settle it in your heart and mind I TRUST GOD! I am the one you should govern your life after. I am your Lord; as your Lord, I am in control. Everything I went through and experienced on the cross was for you. All the physical, emotional pain and social rejection I experienced was all for you, so you would not have too. No, you are not exempt from physical and emotional distress; however, nothing you will ever go through will never compare to what I endured on the cross.*

I honestly, had a moment, where I considered not going to the cross. But I had a nevertheless moment; not my will but, God's will be done. And my assignment was to bridge the relationship between God and man as it was in the beginning. Upon sending me, His only son Jesus, we are now sealed with the Holy Ghost once and for all. Therefore, whosoever will receive Him will never be separated from Him again. You may stray but know I will never leave nor forsake you or the covenant I have with you.

Now we can live life like heaven here on earth. Much like it was in the Garden of Eden. Spend time with me, talk to me and involve me in all that you do. I will perfect those things that concerns you. My words are seed that is planted in your heart which will bring forth a harvest. When you speak my words, it is like a farmer planting a crop. The farmer plants with the expectation to receive a harvest. God's word is the guide to "righteous living. When you sow (speak) His word brings forth a harvest every time. Man knows not how the earth breaks down a hard casing of a seed, but the soil does. The soil knows what to do with a seed when planted. In a little while, the earth will show evidence of what is to come. The

9

transformation has come. A plant blade is no longer a seed, it is evidence, proof of what was planted called manifestation. Because we can see some evidence, it is not harvest time. Keep your faith out there because the harvest is when you could pick corn off the stalk if you planted corn. If beans were planted, then beans should be harvest. When love is planted, you get love. When patience is sown, you harvest patience. When we see a harvest that we do not like, uproot the plant, change the seed and replace it with a desired seed".

The process: Take my word put it in your mouth by saying what I say. Then believe with confidence in God's word. Continue to say with praise and thanksgiving until you see what you have been saying (called watering the seed). Ultimately, you will say what you see. Likewise, as the farmer farms with expectation, we are to also sow, say, see with expectation of God's promised word.

If it is written in His Will, it is yours, take it. For example, you are at a restaurant and they provide the menu. The menu provides you with all the restaurant has to offer. Likewise, let the menu represent the (bible) in your hand, find what you want and place your order. When you go to a restaurant a waiter or waitress ask, what would like from the menu and you reply. If it is not written on the menu, they do not carry it. However, most menu have images to give you an idea of what the food should look like. When the food is served to the table, you will have the etched image in the mind and on the plate. Get an image of what you are believing for and have faith in the words you speak and see the salvation of the Lord bring it to pass. Hallelujah! So, what is it that you want or need from the Lord? Is it written in His Will, Place Your Order!

"The Will"

"Beloved it is my prayer that your faith and trust in me as your Father will be increased as you seek me to supply all your needs. I have given you a life manual (Bible) to reference anything you seek of me to help you in the transition. Listed are a few truths and promises for stirring your faith."

- Call upon me in times of trouble and I will deliver thee... Psalm 50:15.

- There is therefore now no condemnation to them which are in Christ Jesus... Roman 8:1.

- Therefore, if any man be in Christ, he is a new creature, old things are died; behold all things are become new. 2 Corinthians 5:17

- This I say then, walk in the spirit, and ye shall not fulfill the lust of the flesh. Galatians 5:16

- Submit yourselves therefore to God. Resist the devil, and he will flee from you. James 4:7

- The righteous cry, and the Lord hear, and deliver them out of all their troubles. Psalms 34:17

- Fear not; for I am with thee; be not dismayed; for I am thy God; I will strengthen thee, yea I will help thee, I uphold thee with the right hand of my righteousness. Isaiah 41:10

- But ye shall receive power, after the Holy Ghost is come upon you... Act 1:8.

- The Lord shall open unto thee his good treasure, the heaven to give the rain unto thy land in season and to bless all the work of thine hand. You shall lend unto nations and though shall not borrow. Deuteronomy 28:12

- But my God shall supply all your needs according to his riches in glory by Christ Jesus Philippians 4:19

- If my people, which are called by my name shall humble themselves and pray and seek my face and turn from their wicked ways: then will I hear from heaven and will forgive their sin and will heal their land. 2 Chronicles 7:14

- And be ye kind one to another, tenderhearted, forgiving one another, even as God for Christ's sake hath forgiven you. Ephesians 4:32

- When you pray, first forgive anyone you are holding a grudge against, so that your Father in heaven will forgive your sins, too. Mark 11:25

- Trust in the lord with all thine heart; and lean not unto thine own understanding. In all thy ways acknowledge him and he shall direct thy paths. Proverb 3:5-6

- If any of you lack wisdom, let him ask of God, that giveth to all men liberally and upbraided not; and it shall be given to him. James 1:5

- For I will restore health unto thee, and I will heal thee of the wounds, said the Lord... Jeremiah 30:17.

- This is the confidence that we have in him, that, if we ask anything according to his will, he hear us. 1 John 5:14

- For God so love the world, that he gave his only begotten Son, that whosoever believeth in him should not perish, but have everlasting live. John 3:16

- For I am persuaded, that neither death, nor life, nor angels, nor principalities, nor powers, nor things present, nor things to come, nor height, nor depth, nor any other creature, shall be able to separate us from the love of god, which is in Christ Jesus our Lord. Roman 8:38-39

- No weapon that is formed against you shall prosper; and every tongue that shall raise against thee in judgement thou shall condemn. This is the heritage of the servants of the Lord, and their righteousness is of me, said the Lord. Isaiah 54:17

- For I know the plans and thoughts that I have for you, say the Lord, "plans for peace and well-being and not for disaster, to give you a future and a hope. Jeremiah 29: 11

"Change of Identity"

Everyone has an originality to themselves. However, originality is linked to various influences. Identities may be altered due to beliefs, personalities, looks, values, and mindsets. A psychological identity relates to self-image and self-esteem. How you esteem or not esteem yourselves will affect your identity.

Identity should be embraced by what God say about you. Although influences play a role in physical identity, God's influential changes empowers change causing an apparent command to be enforced. After Jesus experience on the cross, He took away the sins of the world and declared Righteousness, but because of what ALL Jesus has done. The identity God has pronounced for humankind is no longer "Sinner." Jesus said, "I am declaring you Righteous". In exchange for receiving me as your Lord. I am changing your identity. You are no longer a sinner. You are my Righteousness, said the Lord!

Let us not be confused, when you feel unworthy or perhaps have behaved in a manner that is not pleasing. Remember these behaviors, and experiences are not your identity and should be handled separately. Simply repent, ask the person and God to forgive you and forgive yourself. This is not the first mistake you have made; you got through it. However, you are aware of the wrong and your conscious reminds you that it is wrong. Therefore, the God in you do not want to live in wrong, so fix it immediately. REPENT, FORGIVE and MOVE ON and (DO NOT) put yourself in that situation again.

Old things have died and tomorrow begins a new day; a new beginning not to make the same mistake again. Since Jesus made you righteous there is nothing you can do to undo your Righteousness. For example, in college you earned a bachelor's degree in a particular field. Upon receiving your degree, you decide to advance educationally by obtaining a master's degree. Would you refer to yourself as having a BA degree or would you refer to your MA? Generally, the highest degree earned is preferred. Even on applications, the highest degree earned is asked first. So likewise, in God's kingdom, there are no sinners' only Righteous men and women. You are 100% Righteous and you do not lose your righteousness when you go outside of God's will. Most decisions have consequences, and the consequence may be harsh, but you are still Righteous with consequences you will have to endure.

Jesus is speaking. *"Upon the date and time on Calvary Hill I spent on the cross, I settled the sin issue for all men from their past, present and future sins. My expectation has and remains that all men come and choose me as their Lord. Because I long to embrace our relationship. So, we can fellowship, laugh, talk, dream, enjoy the love and show compassion one to another as it was in the beginning.*

So, become accustom to your new identity anything other than Righteousness is not talking or referring to you. It is equally important that you do not refer to yourself as much either. Because when you speak against my word it indicates to me one, you do not trust me as Lord. Two, you do not believe nor have faith in me, but you will if you do not give up, quilt and faint. I will continue to do a work in you to transform you from the inside out. Continue to draw near unto me as I draw near to you. Before you know it, you will acknowledge my word is TRUTH."

"Will-Purpose-Destiny"

God's will for the life of the believer is in His Word. He wants everyone to have eternal life, repent and be saved, yet we know everyone will not be saved. It is God's will for all to be healed, yet sickness still robs people of their health. When people are afflicted with illness and they are not healed yet, people have the tendency to blame God. There are many influences that can change the outcome of Gods will. This may be hard to believe, God's will does not automatically come to pass! Starting with your individual will. Every individual is responsible for discovering Gods will. We must decide which will has the strongest influence. Because the strongest will-will determine the path traveled.

For example, you are set to travel to Florida and the time you set is later in the day and God speaks and instructs you to leave now. But you are not quite ready, you have not eaten, and it is too soon. So, you wait and ignore God's will and instruction. It is time to leave and you are stuck in traffic. You have not gotten outside the city limits yet. You are upset and questioning God. God replies, "I told you 3 hours and 15 minutes ago to leave and if you would have obeyed, you would have avoided this delay. Furthermore, you have an additional 2 hours of delay."

Allow God to interrupt your plans because he knows what is best for you. Although His plans are not hidden, we must seek to find it and practice listening for him (Jeremiah 29:12-13). Matthew 7:7 advise us to call, pray, hear, and seek God with all your heart; and you will find. That is good news, Amen.

When you vow and commit to the Lord, we must become Roman 12:1-2. Meaning, we are no longer our own; we belong to God; He purchased us with His blood on that cross. As a reasonable offering of thanksgiving for all He has done; is to give ourselves to Him. Now we must renew the mind to think, say and do as God does. When we do this there will be infallible proof that you are in the Will of God.

How do you know if you are in God's Will?

According to God, His will is His word. When you get His word, understand, and apply his word you are in His will. The Bible is your life manual of reference for anything you need. If by chance you do not find a scripture that connects with your understanding. You can ask the Holy Spirit for help, wisdom to understand your needs. Also, there are many different translations, which can aid you in your discovery. Everything has a name; the Bible's concordance can guide you to relatable scriptures relative to the situation or problem you are dealing with. God will also speak directly to you for your understanding.

For example, the Bible uses parables, illustrations, songs, hymns, dreams, signs, wonders, miracles, to help you understand God and how He operates. However, in this generation, I the Lord will use old and new norms of communication to get your attention.

Today my word is exculpated to show or declare someone is not guilty (free from guilt or blame). Our life experiences have provoked shame, guilt, blame and many negative words that God has not called us nor identified us as being. God's words exculpate (grants us immunity) when applied. Imagine you are mentally and emotionally locked up jailed in shame, guilt, and blame. Upon locating the uplifting scripture, God's word is the Judge who announces (exculpate) freedom and not guilty.

In the book of 1 John 1:9, "if you confess your sin, God is saying He is faithful and just to forgive us from all unrighteousness. This scripture is saying a lot. Let us start with forgive us from all unrighteousness. God is saying it is unrighteous to answer and accept ownership of something that is not yours. That is stealing! Stealing and using it as your own. Who pronounced you as guilty and blamed you for a crime you did not commit? In prior chapters, I addressed your identity. I know what I declared you, said the Lord and it is none of the names you are answering too. God is saying it is unrighteous to answer and accept name contrary to what I your heavenly father has called you. To fix this issue, find and uplifting scripture to meditate on, repent, be thankful and move on. The other issue here demonstrates the love He has for us. He does not leave us the way he found us: drowning in quilt, shame, blame and the things we have wrong. He does not want us to live like that, bound, incarcerated in mind and thoughts or our past. He is saying to us "Come from that place and get in my presence where there is peace, joy, love forevermore".

You are free (exculpated). Jesus was ransom and the debt is paid in full. That is love! Ephesian 5:25-26 "Christ love so that He gave HIMSELF to make you whole, ridding you from the junk, grime, drugs, shame, and sin from of your life.

We are saved now, and we are still looking and acting like Jesus death and resurrection was for nothing. He dealt with the sin issue on the cross. This should not be an issue in believers' lives. This stuff we are dealing with is not considered sin. It is un-renewed minds, unaligned attitudes, behaviors, and habits with consequences. Turn back and read Gods Will again. God's Will is His Word, which says, renew the mind, present yourself as a sacrifice. Now all the issues and emotions you may feel are valid; however, your life should not be governed by your feelings. Whatsoever, God's word says about the topic, that is what you say and believe? God's word washes the mind. Therefore, know this, God is not punishing you because you are experiencing turbulence or unhappiness in your life or because you have glorified your needs and made them greater than God. You are in the wrong the place and looking through the wrong lens. Look at your situation through the eyes of God's Word and get at the feet of Jesus where you will find supernatural peace, joy, and answers. God's blessing and anointing will always grace you to **do** the Will of God for your life and grace will answer during tough situation. Will you listen and obey?

Judge your lives according to the freedoms and delights God has instructed us to have for life. If by chance you find yourself out of alignment with God's plan. Reposition yourself and make the necessary changes to maintain the fruits of the spirit.

When mankind is sure, confident, and established in the authority and dominion provided by God, they can rest assuredly as a man and a woman in **Oneness** with God. Knowing the will, purpose, and destiny for their lives.

Will= God's Word

Purpose=Carry out God's legacy, *Living After Death* using the ministry gift tools to cultivate intimacy and accomplish anything you are graced to do in line with God's Will.

Destiny= Eternal Lifelong journey fulfilling God's will and purpose for your life both in heaven and here on the earth.

"Exculpate"

The word *exculpate* is a rhema word from the Lord. As I was writing about the will, purpose and destiny, the Lord said my word is often used to exculpate the people. I was astonished with the word; it was not in my vocabulary and I had never heard of it before and I could not spell the word. So, I asked God to spell the word and He did. I immediately, gathered all the reference tools to find the meaning. I was so excited with joy that He trusted me with this word. Therefore, I felt compelled to expound it further.

Exculpate is a Latin word defined as absolve, exonerate, acquit, vindicate mean to free from a charge, from blame. It implies a clearing from blame or fault often in a matter of small importance to clear from blame.

I heard the Lord say my word is used to exculpate people. My word sets people free. People are mentally and emotionally incarnated with blame, shame, and guilt because of the choices they made and experiences. They do not see themselves as I see them. Their views are distorted with worthlessness, un-forgiveness of self and shame. God says, His word exonerates and vindicate the shame, guilt, blame, and feeling not worthy. God says, you are not guilty in my eyes. For I have set you free from bondage, slavery, incarnation of the mind, emotions, and negative thoughts. All which are lies. Stop believing the lies and stop trying to relate your behavior as your identity because you are not your behavior!

If you are still holding fast to the experiences that have kept you bound, it is clear your mind is not renewed in God's word, and there is a lack of trust. The continuous acts of guilt, shame and blame are very dangerous to a believer, because 2 Timothy 4:3 mentions a time coming when people will not endure sound teaching but having itching ears, they will accumulate for themselves teachings to suit their own passions. This behavior reminds me of someone mentally bound in slavery, and are set free and do not walk out of the cell of escape. In the book of John 16:8-10, (Passion Translation) says *when he comes, he will expose sin and prove that the world is wrong about sin and righteousness and his judgement: about sin, because people refuse to believe in who I am; about righteousness, because I am going to the Father, where you can see me no longer.*

"Not withholding my word as TRUTH is an abomination said the Lord." You must commit to my ways or not. Meaning you must decide to be hot for God or cold for the devil not lukewarm. John records in Revelation 3:15-16 "I know your works, that you are neither cold nor hot. I wish you were cold or hot. "So then, because you are neither cold nor hot, but lukewarm, I will spew you out of my mouth. God wants you to be cold or hot because with this sureness comes hope. He can convert, transform, and change the hot or cold. The lukewarm is double minded and unstable in all his ways. (James 1:8)

This scripture reference can view lukewarm as a believer who enjoys the benefits of God Grace by day and still dances with the devil and all its impurities by night. The lukewarm person is delusional, mentally, and emotionally unstable, confused, and in a constant battle pulling to and from like tug-a-war.

Commit unto the Lord! His word is proven truth, and He has already set you free. Yes, it may be uncomfortable when you have been operating under a different system. It is not uncommon to be apprehensive, but trust God. There is so much to gain by following His guidance instead of trusting in our own.

Have you ever traveled to a place where you have never been before while driving? You trust the GPS as your guide. The only way you can get there is by the mercy of the GPS. Do not let the GPS signal drop. You may become in a state of panic, traveling in circles, and ultimately lost. It is a great tool to use and is on point most of the time. You rely on its accuracy. Just like you trust the GPS, trust God even when you do not know where you are going. Rely on Him. Involve Him in all that you do. If He said you are exculpated, walk in the freedom of deliverance from shame, blame and guilt.

He loves you and wants the best for you. You must believe that beyond any doubt.

Exculpate frees us from the mental anguish, of learned experiences, knowledge and philosophy taught over the course of years, which have patterned and governed our lives. Therefore, if anyone is in Christ, he has a new life. Put off the old self, which belongs to your former corrupt manners of life, and be renewed in the spirit of your mind. Put on the coat of Righteous created just for you after the likeness of God in true righteousness and holiness. Ephesians 4:22-24.

"What is man that though are mindful of him?"

Spirit Soul and Body

Before you were born, I knew you. I made you in my image as tripartite spirit, soul, and body. The body was formed from the dust of the ground and God breath the breath of life into man. Mankind <u>became </u>a living being with all three parts spirit, soul, and body Genesis 2:7.

Before becoming alive man was mere dust of the ground, a breathless being. Without salvation we are walking dead, 2-part man (Adam), (soul and body) existing and alive functioning from learned, acquired knowledge, experiences, and influences.

Through grace by faith, we receive salvation unto righteousness, we then <u>become </u>Spirit, Soul and Body. We are a spirit; we process a soul, and we live in a body. We became tripartite being upon receiving Jesus. 1 Corinthian 15:45 says, "the first Adam became a living being. The last Adam (Jesus) became life giving spirit.

John 16:7-13 the spirit we are born with is the breath of life (first Adam) and that is why we can live. You are alive, yet without Christ and are denied access to the covenant promises of grace, which are in the Will of God.

The Holy Spirit (life giving Spirit) will transform us into a new being-a being which God will live forever. I Thessalonians 5:23, Knowing this, living by the Spirit becomes paramount in the lives to those who believes. Galatians 5:25 declares, if we live by the Spirit, let us also behave in accordance with the spirit. The Spirit of God replaces the sinful nature that once rebelled against God. Why? To reestablish Himself as the new ruling prince of our life.

This change in ruler-governorship is permeated by the character of the spirit. This change is taking ownership of the Spirit of Grace (work free). Though we were once dead to God, we are now alive together in Him. We are God's workmanship created in Christ Jesus.

Imagine our renewed mind as the Holy Ghost hovers over us and Jesus saying let there be... and there was. Just as God said in the beginning, let there be as the Holy Ghost hovered over the earth as he commanded, so it was. As you speak the word of God from a renewed mindset, you too can say, let there be, and it became. What have you said lately, and it came to pass shortly thereafter? That is the glory of living by the spirit. What an awesome experience to recognize God working through you as another speaking spirit in the earth. When you see a dark situation and you operate in faith and authority calling those things that be not as though they were (Romans 4:17), activates change, setting in motion transformation. Wow! Mankind who knows his authority, exercises that authority in faith according to the Will of God is someone to behold. What is Man that though are mindful of him?

A man (speaking spirit) who sees in the spirit, says in the natural what he sees. Then he will continue to say what was seen in the spirit until he sees it in the natural. This is faith manifested from the spirit to the natural. It is by this gift of Grace that the new life we live in the spirit is one not gratifying the desires of the flesh. Living by the spirit is not being controlled by satisfactions, powers. prestige and world pleasures. Galatians 5:17 states the flesh will produce one kind of desire and the spirit produces another kind and they are in opposition of each other. Walking by the spirit is a demonstration of the Word of God in action, which is ultimately living by the spirit. Another example, In Romans 7:18 where Paul acknowledges that in himself his flesh is no good, apart from the Grace of God. His flesh, mind, and thoughts are subject to his perversions, learned behaviors and experiences. However, Roman 8:7 says, new desires are generated from love, yearning, and longing. When the desires for love (doing the right thing) is stronger than the flesh, we walk in victory over the fleshly desires.

Therefore, walking in the spirit enables us to do in accordance with God's will, says the Lord. Ezekiel 36:26-27 "A new heart and new spirit I will put within you... I will cause you to walk in my statutes.

This next topic ties in with each other, which will help us understand the difference between living by the spirit and not living according to the law.

"Led by the Spirit not By the Law."

Galatians 5:18 says, "But if you are led by the spirit you are not under the law."

Paul shifts his teaching from "walking by the spirit to being led by the spirit". Being led by the spirit is determined by who is governing, the stronger spirit, if you will. God's spirit leads us by creating desires to obey, comply, and align our thinking, our words and we walk by fulfilling those actions, God's way. Now being led by the law has a condemnation, blame, worthless, shame, guilt, residue tag attached, which is often in the fine print. Evidence of the law causes you to question your identity and faith as though God has never done anything for you and gone to the cross to redeem you. The law demands the burden of proof upon you to do something to earn, deserve, or qualify for God's Grace.

Settle in your heart the Grace of God, His Righteousness, and covenant promises are all gifts. Our responsibility is to receive.

However, as you are reading and renewing your mind, always ask yourself is this a gift, or do I have to work for it? Receive everything God has for you. It is your inheritance as stated in the will. However, if you must earn it, or do something to gain possession then it is a law issue. YOU ARE NOT UNDER THE LAW! YOU ARE UNDER GRACE! SAY IT! I AM UNDER GRACE, Not the law.

Remember the fine print, the law condemns, blames, and will have you thinking you are not enough, not worthy. It will remind you of the past or the last time you messed up. Do not fall for that nonsense, you are redeemed from the curse of the law and made righteous through and by the shedding of the Blood of Jesus Christ.

When you are reminded of your past sins, that is the time to open your mouth and use the authority God gave you. Put the word of God (weapon) on your lips and say, "I am redeemed from the curse of the law." "I cast down any imagination, thought that does not line up with God's word". Declare your redemption and victory over the situation. Do not meditate on negative thoughts that taunt your spirit. Bless God! Silence those thoughts and suggestions, most importantly, resist, reject any condemning words that are spoken to you, over you and rehearsed mentally.

Victory is sweet when you become skilled in using the authority you have in Christ. Just like when a boxer TKO his opponent. What! Next! Bring It! Thank you, Jesus, for the VICTORY!

We can never take the credit or boast for the victory because we are nothing within ourselves, we could not have done it alone. In Him we live, in Him we breathe, in Him we have our very being (Act 17:28). Thanks be to God who causes us to be triumph in all things (2 Corinthians 2:14).

Have you ever made a deal, or a promise to God for selfish desires or gains, of which, we feel incapable of attaining through self-works? We ask God to grant us favor and to cosign on something that will lead to our demise or destruction are all perpetuated acts of the law. God does not and will not respond to anything that is not in his will. Therefore, when disappointment and rejection knock at your door after your failed plan attempts, you began to blame God for not answering your prayers. News Flash! He only answers to His words. Wrong number if you think God is in the bartering business or in the let us make a deal business. You do not know your God. Go back and read His will.

We do not have to earn God's blessing nor love for us. He freely gives it to us without bargain tactics.

"The integrity of My Word"

God Speaking: *"Value my word. It is the same word I used to create the Heavens and the earth.*

You trust the words of music, opinions, and gossip and never fact check to see if it is true before you spread and share with others.

Yet, my living Word is the world best kept secret in your world. Who are you sharing me with?

I have demonstrated, given you examples, used parables, metaphors, and illustrations for you to believe and receive my word. What is the problem?

All I want is a relationship with you. You can trust me, believe me, and have faith in me. I am better than the closest person to you. There is nothing outside my word that I have not or will not provide for you.

I would think my word is sufficient. My Word is the tool that can speak life or death, reach deep within the bone morrow to save what is mine. There is nothing, no place too high, too low, too wide, too deep to separate me from you. Can you say the same?

I am so into you that a mere hand raise of praise gets heaven attention and satisfies my soul with a fragrance of joy and pleasure. You are always on my mind! I perfect those things which concerns you. Before you can complete a thought, I already know the inner most secrets, thoughts, and desires of your heart."

I Get Jealous!

God Speaking: Put no other God before me! I get jealous when others spend more time with you than the time you spend with me.

Do not let your emotions govern or rule your life, that is my place. You have become so emotional driven that your hearing becomes dull to my voice. You question if I am present and you know I have told you that I will never leave or forsake you.

Then your discerner is off, and you cannot distinguish my voice from your thinking. An adjustment is needed. Simply go back to the Will (my Word).

You are out of alignment and the pain, stress, and cloudy judgements will all continue if you allow your emotions to govern your life.

We live by faith in the Word of God. It is paramount to live by my word. If we are not living according to my Word, we are walking dead. Choose which you will be, alive in Christ or alive to sin.

To be completely honest, I am extremely jealous for you. You see, I have pledged, promised, and covenant with you and presented you as a pure virgin to the Anointed One. But now I am afraid that history will repeat itself. Just as that serpent tricked Eve with his wiles, so your hearts and minds will be tricked, and you will stray from my love and devotion. So, when someone comes and presents themselves different from what you know of my spirit and my Word, you receive that spirit and go with it without fact checking and declare it as your truth. 2 Corinthians 11:2-4 (The Voice).

Do not leave me, abandon me, do not throw away what we have built together, I LOVE YOU!

"God Love you so much"

"You are not your behavior nor emotions".

The imperfection of our nature will cause us to misjudge situations, make mistakes and experience trials and tribulations. Some of which are self-inflected others are inflected upon us. Yet, we are to repent, forgive and move on.

Stop with the emotional whip of guilt, shame, low esteem and questioning your identity. Did you forget, you are the righteousness of God. You must separate who you are from the circumstances or turns of events. Making a mistake, missing the mark does not change your identity or God's love for you. Yet, we become vested in the negative emotions because of disappointments. Do not wear negative emotions from trials as a coat, nor take ownership by changing your name. For example, feeling guilty because I failed to do something. You were righteous before you failed to do something. You are righteous even afterward. Keep the righteous coat on and go back and correct what you failed to do. They are not the same and your righteousness is not on trial when you mess up, so stop making it an issue.

The coat of righteousness is love, joy, peace, forgiving, meekness, and knowing that God is a deliverer, help in a time of trouble. Call on the Lord He is your refuge, fortress, your God in whom you can depend. Be the Psalms 91.

Learn to forgive yourself as you ask others to forgive you.

God gave us emotions to express and connect with all his creation. So, we might know aw, surprise, breathtaking beauty, taste, feelings, joy, happiness, sad, touch, smell and much more. Imagine not having any emotions, we could not appreciate the sun's beauty reflecting on the ocean at sunset as the vibrant colors dance on the waves. We could not appreciate the beauty of flowers and the amazing fragrance they release into the atmosphere if we did not have emotions.

However, emotions are not standards for living and governing our lives. We must feel and acknowledge what is felt but respond God's way. There have been times in my life that I became so angry that I wanted to put my hands on somebody, but I did not respond in the manner of my emotions. I chose to (sin not) simply walk away. Put a bridle over my mouth. Re-aligned my emotions and speak in tongues putting the word of God on my lips. I prayed and offered thanksgiving unto the Lord for delivering me out of what could have been a mess.

The consequences for reacting out of the emotions is very costly, unpredictable, and damaging to self and others. The reactions will not resemble holiness nor the kingdom. The difference is the God in me changed the course of my action. Whereas, without Christ the outcome would have been different, and the consequences could have caused a chain reaction (fired, assault charges, lawsuit… loss of income, health insurance ….) in my life as well as those involved. Which outcome would you prefer? I choose to follow Christ.

"Know your Covenant"

Live by and rely on your covenant with God. Know your God and your covenant with Him. Because when you know that you know, you are mighty men and women of God who can do great exploits in the Name of Jesus.

I am sure you have a skill set that you are very confident with and you have mastered the craft. You do not have to brag or boast, because your work speaks for itself. Likewise, be confident in your covenant relationship with God, crediting Him for your success and your ability to do.

I like David's tenacity I Samuel 17: 26, 27 where he tells King Saul "Who is this uncircumcised Philistine, that he should defy the armies of the living God... The Lord that delivered me out of the paw of the lion and out of the paw of the bear, he will deliver me out of the hand of this Philistine."

If the Lord has EVER delivered you out of anything, boast in the Lord for that, because He is a deliverer, a way maker, a healer…a provider.

I love sports, but not more than my God. However, if we would boast about God's covenant, as we do about perhaps our favorite football team, imagine the great things our heavenly father will allow for us.

The covenant we have with God is unbreakable and guaranteed. It is a better covenant than that which Abram had. Abram's covenant required animal blood sacrifices with laws that could not be broken unless declared cursed. Thanks be to God, the blood Jesus shed on the cross was for all eternity, and no animal blood can remove my sin stains. Nothing but the blood of Jesus. What can make me whole again, nothing but the blood of Jesus?

Though we have been found guilty of breaking the covenant, we are free from the curse of the law and judged not guilty. We must know that God loves us without a shadow of doubt, and He is covenant minded. The covenant is ever before Him, and He does not forget the promises He has made. If He said it, He would bring it to pass. Become fully persuaded that God loves you and He wants to fulfill every covenant promise He said in His word.

Jesus took your sin and gave you righteousness. He has become one with you. He took your weakness and gave you His strength. When we encounter life battles, we are naturally weak within our own strength. The Christ in you the hope of glory, fights for you and equips you with heavenly armor so you can stand, and nothing penetrates your armor. Ephesians 6:10, 11, 13-17 describes the heavenly armor and its functions, that's covenant. What battle have you experienced before Christ that gave you tools and tells you to stand? None, before Christ everything was a weapon of opportunity. Whatsoever I could put my hands to, was used to defend myself. But, not your loving father, who knows and sees far beyond what can be seen in front of you. That is why we must trust and depend upon Him. Because being strong in the power of His might can save us from ourselves and the consequences that lie ahead. Therefore, be exuberant concerning your covenant and allow Him to be Lord over your life.

In a metaphoric manner, knowing your covenant is like you knowing your checkbook. You have an expectation that your direct deposit will be deposited on payday like clockwork. You can access that account as often as needed for as long as something is there. When you run low on funds, you make a deposit. Do you see where I am going? Lets' let the checking account represent your covenant. You know exactly what rights and privileges you have in Christ Jesus and you can access it as needed. The beauty of this covenant account is unlimited funds never runs low. All transactions represent ownership and confidence to make withdrawals and deposits at will. And when your account runs low, your spiritual account is never low, and you can deposit the Word to build your faith account to continue making withdraws whenever needed from God.

The expectation of your money being in the bank on time is the same expectation we should have towards your covenant. Expect God to deliver whatever you need because he is accessible immediately.

"Cultivate the Relationship with God"

Relationship is work. Regardless of who the relationship is with, you are going to have to do the work. Work more than you prefer, in ways you do not prefer and at times it is inconvenient. Nevertheless, we must choose to embrace our relationships intentionally to move from too little or too much communication, honesty, commitment, time, and vulnerability.

For example, cultivating and maintaining relationships is like selfcare to a healthy body. As you may well know the human body requires maintenance. The complexity of our beautiful bodies indicates when something is too little or too much. Too little water, sleep, exercise. Too much sun, food, pain. The unique specimens of the body calibrate inflammation, disease, headache, stomach irritation, etc. You get the idea. Cultivating and maintaining a healthy relationship with God's house start with maintaining a healthy body.

According to 1 Corinthians 6:19 *the body is the temple of the Holy Spirit who is in you, whom you have received from God?* Therefore, we must do what is necessary to maintain good strong healthy bodies for the long haul. Eat right, exercise, reduce stress, get regular checkups and dental visits, eye exams, get plenty of rest, hygiene, grooming, reduce risky behaviors. This is how we cultivate a Godly relationship with our body.

How to connect spiritually with God is to know God. Know Him as sovereign Lord, not just the Lord of the universe. Know Him personally in which he leeds, and we follow. Psalms 100:3 T*ells us to know that the Lord is God. It is He who made us, and we are His.* It further tells us how to go to God, in verse 4 of 100 Psalm, enter His presence with thanksgiving and praise giving thanks for He is good, and His love endures forever.

To know Him is to know His Word, Will, Plan and destiny for your life. Jeremiah 29:11 For I know the plans I have for you," "plans to prosper you and not to harm you, plans to give you hope and a future. In a relationship with God, we can take comfort in Jeremiah 29:11 knowing God has a plan for our lives regardless of situations, hardships or crisis we face. Know the plans, He has for you involves seeking guidance and answers from Him. God uses many ways to communicate with you to ensure your understanding. Revealed knowledge through the Word of God, dreams, speaking, prophesy, in prayer and parables. Parables were used to reveal and conceal truth. No need to worry because Jesus concealed truth from those who would reject his message. As believers, He revealed the truth withholding nothing. In seeking Him, He will reveal the truth through revealed knowledge, insightful discovery, zeal for more and rightfully dividing the Word of truth from commentary. Trust me God knows how to get your attention and communicate with you best. The eyes of your understanding are enlightened, your ears are anointed to hear the message behind what is being read or spoken. Spending time reading the bible you gain access to knowledge of Him. How He values the covenant He made with us. He further says, He watches His Word to perform it. So, as you use His Words in faith according to His promises, He will perform and bring it to pass. It is not our job nor responsibility to be God over our lives, That's God job! It is our responsibility to have and maintain the integrity of His Word, believe, receive, trust, and have faith in what He said. In all things, I trust God.

I like to use Mark chapter 4 in conveying the integrity of God's Word via parable. The Parable of the Sower gives us a realistic example of a farmer who plants seeds in the ground and the seed produces a harvest. Likewise, is the Word of God, when the Word of God is planted (spoken) in your heart, it will produce a harvest. Although, many say they are confused or do not understand with parables. Yes, the mind cannot comprehend what the ground does when a seed is planted, but the ground knows exactly what to do and how to transform a hard casein of a seed to produce a tree. Another example when fertilization takes place with an ovum and sperm it produces a human. Man knows not how two bodily fluids can produce a human, but it does. So, what am I saying, there will be many things in life that you will not understand, but it happens? You must trust the integrity of God's Word as truth. As this parable indicates the working of the Kingdom of God, the Word must be planted in your heart so growth can come. In planting there are stages: the blade, the ear, then the full corn ear. In human body stages: infant, toddler, adolescent, teen, young adult, adult. In Spirit, plant seed -Word of God, *hope, faith*, and *manifestation*. This is how God's word is released into our lives.

Prayer is another way to cultivate a relationship with God. But it is more than getting our request answered. 1 John 5:14-15 *This is the confidence we have in approaching God: that if we ask anything according to his will, he hears us. And if we know that he hears us whatever we ask we know that we have what we asked of him.*

Prayer is ultimate fulfillment, it expresses a need and want of Him not necessarily in receiving only, but assurance and sustainability in the relationship with God that everything is alright. Praying should never be associated, as being a waste of time. A prayer is communicating with God in an intimate way knowing I have someone to depend upon. So, to pray is to secure and sustain the relationship with God when you do not know what to do and knowing what to do with assurance and thanksgiving.

To start praying, imaging Jesus as a close friend you trust who does not judge you for what you are experiencing. Just talk to

Him. Talk from a place of unloading His words and needing His help. Although He knows what you are going through even before you speak. Continue talking to him and after you finish, LISTEN! Listening is a powerful skill set to have in your relationship with God. Because He is always speaking. Often, we are not listening. We allow spoken words to pass over us and not give attention to it until something happens, or it is too late, then we will say, something told me. That something was the voice of God warning you of what lies ahead.

It is easy to get caught up in how to pray ...what to pray. Is there a correct way to pray? We may see and hear how others pray and judge yourself accordingly. Simply, tell God what is on your heart and listen to His loving, assuring, comforting words. Sometimes God can be very direct and chastising depending on the request and behavior, attitude, and unrenewed mind response. Know this, all is done in love.

I remember emphatically when I began to increase my listening skills, it was after the 9-11 tragedy. I read and heard news report from people saying, their routine was changed, something told them not to go to work, perhaps delayed for some apparent reason. I believe God spoke to everyone that day but not everyone was listening. Even after listening some did not obey.

After that tragic experience, I began to train my ears to hear and listen to my spirit speak in crowded environments. I began changing my morning habits by turning off the radio. It has been stated, if any body organs are lost, the others are enhanced or compensate. As I practiced listening my eyes became more focused, where I could see things in the spirit as clear as I could hears in the spirit. The Lord began showing me people, things, how to orchestrate lessons and He allowed me to see things I knew nothing about which prompted me to pray and intercede for others.

For example, I remember traveling this route to work daily where there was usually a lot of traffic and often there would be a man standing on the corner with a sign. I could not read the sign because it was early and dark. One morning, while driving to work, I heard the Lord say as I prepared to exit, to give the man at the end of the street $5. I did not know if the man was on the corner, or if I had the money, because I generally do not carry cash on me. So, I dug through the purse trying to locate $5 mind you, there was usually heavy traffic this time of the morning, however not so this morning. I found $5 wrapped in a receipt and gave it to the man with no one in sight. After giving the man…money I continued to drive, I could not help but ponder, what was the conversation with the man and God, prior to my arrival. I traveled this direction daily. The man was on this corner mostly every morning. Prior to this morning, the Lord did not speak to me concerning the man nor instructed me to do anything. What happened? Why did God tell me to give this man money before I saw the man and without knowing if I had money to give? Perhaps I was tested to see if one I heard and two if I would obey. If that was my test for the day, I passed. There were so many experiences that took place and still exist how the Lord would yield information and prompt me to action.

In cultivating a Godly relationship through prayer, be anxious for nothing, but in prayer and supplication let your request be make known unto God, and with thanksgiving without worrying (Philippians 4:6-7). Rather than worry pray. It is best not to pray if you are worrying, because worry is a form of fear. Fear that what you prayed will not be heard nor come to pass. Maybe you did not believe what you prayed; you were just venting to God. God hears everything only responds to His Word, so when we pray God's Word He will answer. Praying the problem does not yield faith in God's Word. Rehearsing the problem in the name of prayer may lead to unanswered prayers, frustration, blame God and out of frustration becomes dishearten with God. That is not an ideal place to be in when feeling empty, void, and hopeless. Having thoughts of God not listening and answering your prayers is not healthy and a clear indicator your emotions are ruling. That type of thinking leads to trust issues guilt, shame, disappointment, regret, unforgiveness a string of negative reactions of which are not the Will of God.

However, if defaulted to the Word of God, the response and outcome will be different without the negativity links. What does that mean to default to the Word of God? Everything you will encounter has a name. Look in the bible concordances and see what God's Word say about that word and do what it said, say what it says as it relates to His promises. In other words, duplicate, imitate the things of God. Today, when we want to find out information, Google university is the way most people seek answers. Key words are input, and a host of information comes up. You then must decipher truth from commentary. The Word of God is truth, we must rightly divide the Word of truth in context of events and context as applied to our lives.

To Know God through personal experience. Early in life, most have been trained, educated of self-care of the body, perhaps not as much care in relationships. In relationship, trial and error are the teachers, knowing what to do, what to say, the tone in which it is said or written, how our words, attitudes, behaviors matter and affect others. All are rooted from personal experiences.

Personal experience with God is rooted and grounded in His love for us even if we have not loved Him. 1 John 4:10 records it this way, "In this is love, not that we love God, but that He loved us."

According to Acts 17: 27, God is not far from us, so that they who seek the Lord, in the hope they will find Him. This is an example of God's love for mankind, all of creation was made for our inhabitation and enjoyment. God determined the exact times and places where we should live. So, men would seek him and perhaps reach out for him and find him because he is not far away. In the past God overlooked the ignorance of man designed idols, now He is commanding all people to repent. We have been in the dark too long about God and the resurrection of Jesus. God has revealed Himself through some personally, and through others vicariously. Let us stop denying God and His son Jesus and all that He endured on the cross for us. The indication of our choices to deny, resist and ignore God is spiritual separation. How can you partake of the Will of someone when you reject the benefactor?

Jesus is telling us, "I am the way, the truth and the life. No one comes to the Father except through Me." (John 14:6)

"Living After Devastation."

Life is filled with various events which cause hurt, pain, and disappointments. Often left feeling empty, abandoned, guilty, and ashamed. Surprisingly, the body does not know the difference between the pain from a divorce, death, nor disappointments. Because the body response is the same. The body releases endorphins and adrenaline throughout the body causing the muscles to contract and produce additional blood flow in specific areas. When these endorphins adrenaline is released, the body responds with elevated heart rates and blood pressures, sweating, headache, anxiety, nausea, and it incite emotions. Emotions of shock, anger, fear, hurt, rage, violence, hatred, etcetera. These emotions are displayed with a response, which is key to any situation. How we respond emotionally is predicated upon the outcome of the condition. I believe emotions are discrete and fundamentally different by individuals biological processes. Because the characteristics attached to each emotion expressed vary in degrees, which emotion is valued, expressed, and regulated. The frequency of emotions are circumstantial in which they are expressed.

Furthermore, we should be able to identify what emotion a person is feeling and the dimensional intensity by facial expressions, body gestures and tones. Although there may be dimensional facial expressions, emotions which cause an arousal is somewhat responsible for the affects. The affects are sometime referred to as triggers, stimuli, and stressors.

Emotions are authentic and expressible, which can be evoked or directed toward specific objects and people. However, how your life should not be governed by the expression of your emotions, arousals, pleasures, and displeasures.

As a believer, I have grown to control my emotions most of the time. However, when devastation hits, my response is different. I have experienced many devasting events in my life, from death, brokenhearted, divorce, falsely accused, opening the door to abandonment, disappointment, shame, guilt, worthlessness. I wish I could tell you there is a fix all process, but I cannot. As I mentioned earlier, individual biological processes yield different results at different time allotments. I cannot factually state the exact time it will take to get beyond hurts, neither can I measure the depth of the pain. What I can say, is there is help, and comfort throughout the process, if desired.

There are many reasons to seek comfort, and peace, because you just want the devastation rehearsal to be over and the emotional rollercoaster to stop. People look for comfort in things, places, food and drinks, people, and rest.

In things, I have found retail therapy to be helpful; not spending what I do not have. Although, I have filled the shopping cart with clothing and after trying them on, returned everything back to the racks, purchasing nothing. That comfort was temporal, though it took my mind off the mental anguish, I was able to transfer those emotions to positive self-esteem. That comfort was short lived and had little sustainability. So, I called on my helper, The Holy Spirit to HELP ME! I knew that whatsoever I asked the Father he would help and give me an answer. I found in the WORD that he heals a broken heart. My heart was broken into pieces and I needed a Master to put me back together. I looked up every brokenhearted scripture and became intimate with the Word, so much so, I could literally feel Him stroking my hair as I laid in his bosom. Every tear drop was caught in His hand. I was assured that as the journey continued, I knew I was not alone, and God comforted me. Therefore, I was encouraged and strengthen to go on in Him with these scriptures: Psalm 147:3, Revelation 21:4, 1 Corinthians 13:7, John 14:27, Matthew 11:28-30, Philippians 4:13 name a few.

I was further encouraged through inspirational gospel music by Yolanda Adams with songs like: *In the Midst of It All, Fragile Heart, Never Give Up, The Battle Is the Lords, Open My Heart.*

In places, I wanted to get to the water. A physical body of water like a lake, ocean, pond, where I could experience serenity without thinking. Often, the closest I could get to water were my tears. Crying is a common action triggered by different emotions. I came to realize my tears released stress, toxins and helped my body to rest and digest both physical and emotional pain. After a good cry I would feel lighter and my spirits were lifted. Each crying episode, left me feeling renewed, refreshed until I began to time my pity parties. I timed myself for one minute to revisit the pain until there was a resistance. I resisted and rejected the mentally and emotionally rehearsing of the pain. I began to look at the situation through a different set of lenses. Through the lens of God. Seeing my life through His view was greater, better than my fogged distorted view. I began with thanksgiving. What? Yes, thanksgiving. I was thankful for the journey, the relocation, opportunity, relationships rather than focus on what was no more. Perhaps if you had children in the relationship, thank God for the gift of your children, not regretting the selection of their father or mother. Instead, be thankful, because in that relationship there were growths, experiences, opportunities and more all to strengthen and develop you as a man or a woman. This is where the scriptures of 1 Thessalonians 5:18 became alive in my life. *Give thanks in all circumstances; for this is the will of God in Christ Jesus for you.* Prior to the awakening of this scripture, I remember asking myself, how can you be thankful in pain, hurt, devastation, death, divorce. Prior to the Holy Spirit unveiling Himself in the Word, I could only see my pain. He showed me how my experiences were pathways to an expected end. Seeing through His lens, opened my eyes and I could see with clarity. I am reminded of the scripture where it talks about the people had eyes to see, but they could not see, ears to hear, but could not hear Isaiah 6:9-10, Acts 28:27. Before seeing with clarity, I was fixated on the problem and I could not see the solution, rather because I was hurting, I wanted others to hurt as well. That was not God's outlook for this situation. He wanted me to know, just as He hung on the cross, endured physical torture, emotional shame public embarrassment, and feeling forsaken, in all these things I will never experience the degree of pain He encountered. And despite the suffering, He focused on the assignment and thank God to have finished. To know His plot and reasonings, I am Thankful, and I find tranquility in Psalm 91. With emphasis on verses one and two, *"He who dwells in the secret place of the Most High shall abide under the shadow of the Almighty. I will say of the Lord, "He is my refuge and my fortress My God, in Him I will trust."*

In comfort of people: When situations and circumstances happen, I default to God. Looking unto Him for my help because all my help comes from the Lord. Now, I have not always defaulted to God. I tried self-resolutions operating in my own strength and knowledge. Sometimes reaching out to friends and family for comfort. Nevertheless, I needed something spiritual. Sharing with family often became frustrating because, family would respond out of their love for me, causing more emotional hype and counselors instead of spiritual counselors that I needed. They became so emotionally involved; I had to spiritually walk them off the ledge. Have this happened to you before? So, you learn how to gauge what and how much information you need to share with others to keep yourself in a peaceful place.

The comfort I needed was in His presence. In His presence was peace, love, intercession, compassion. According to Romans 8:26, *The spirit helps in our weakness. For we do not know what we should pray for as we ought, but the Spirit Himself makes intercession for us with groanings which cannot be uttered".*

When you go to people, family, and friends for counsel, feeling like no one understands and your hardship goes unnoticed, it is important to know who you unload on because being on the same spiritual frequency can feed your spirit for comfort and any other frequency may impact the situation negatively the more. Therefore, take you burdens to the Lord, *the Father of mercies and God of all comfort, who comforts us in all our afflictions, so that we may be able to comfort those who are in any affliction, with the comfort with which we ourselves are comforted by God.* 2 Corinthians 1:3-4

Last, comfort in Rest: Rest in the finish works of Jesus. "It is Finished!" Everything you will every encounter is found in Him. The instructions are simple, He said, Come and receive rest. Walk with me, learn from me, and find rest. I like Mark 6:31 where he advises, "Come away by yourselves to a desolate place and rest a while." For many were coming and going, and they had no leisure even to eat. Does that describe your life? We have become so busy in doing, busy about being busy. We carry many of life hurries, we push ahead and try to keep pace throughout seasons. Stop It! Everything resets and starts anew except you. Allow yourself to reset, rejuvenate, refresh, reconnect, be reliable, be resourceful and relate. Even in sleep, you never turn your brain off. The subconscious and conscious of the brain is constantly working. Just like your computer. Closing the lid is not turning off the computer. Even a computer needs to be turned off to get new updates and downloads after a hard day of work. What about you? Truths, rest is vitally essential. It will either take the rest or you will yield to rest. Rest taken will put you in a situation where you will not have a choice. Therefore, choose the Sabbath. Rest in His promises and live, which is the Will of God. Selah

"Living After Corona"

In 2020, what can be said about how to live after the infectious deathly Coronavirus pandemic. Between the global protest, economic shutdown, systemic bias, and racism, it is an undertaking. This crisis is affecting everyone differently, none the less profoundly. There is only one way to get through this and that is to believe on the Lord Jesus Christ and trust in His finished works. The finish works of protection, deliverance, healing, safety, provider, good health, prosperous life, comforter of the Holy Spirit, prayer and intersession, and foresight. These are sure things of the Spirit that must be exercised daily during these difficult times.

To get through these perilous times physically, mentally, and emotionally-is to rest. Controlling the thoughts and emotions fueled by circumstances and bad behavior of others. Adhere to guidelines for safety of self and others. *Be anxious for nothing, but in everything by prayer and supplication, with thanksgiving, let your request be made known to God; and the peace of God, which surpasses all understanding, will guard your hearts and minds through Christ Jesus.* Philippians 4:6-8

Do what you know to do to maintain good health and reduce the risk. Life must have significance to you to live meaningfully. Living as a Christian changes your attitude on how situations are viewed. Previously without Christ I lived without hope or expectation, but now I have new hope in my heart.

In this crisis, I believe God saturates all people with His Spirit to show His grace and mercy. His grace is sufficient, and we will be able to deal with the problems of this virus optimistically which I believe will take one's faith to new dimension in Him. I am reminded of a time after the parting of the Red Sea. There was not a health pandemic, but people were displaced, experiencing something they have never experienced before. Yet the Lord took care of them. That same God is taking care of mankind in 2020. God's grace is demonstrated during this pandemic. No doubt this crisis has left a devastating effect on many people, making it difficult to face their fears optimistically. There is hope in Jesus one can find rest for their souls in a new assured manner if we believe.

What Will you Do?

"A Renewed Life" is a limitless, powerful, supernatural life through the Holy Spirit. Take the Word of God and apply it to our everyday lives following the guidance of the Holy Spirit, which leads, guides, teaches and directs us through our daily walk with Christ.

Take the posture of Thanksgiving. Thanking God for merely waking us up, good health, strong mind, wisdom, protection and for the help of the Holy Spirit. When situations occur in our lives as they sometime will, the fact you came out is evidence of His Grace and Mercy. You can now say, God is a deliverer, and you can testify of that.

Now everything we read in the Bible is not pertaining to us. What? I thought you said the bible is our life manual. Yes, that is true. The bible is inspired by God for our learning. We can learn from the recorded experiences without experiencing them firsthand.

Besides there are rituals, laws, religion practices, old covenant that are obsolete, void and is not applicable.

However, reading the bible is purpose driven, specific to what you seek. As babes in Christ as well as seasoned believers, you must read the bible from the lens of before Christ and after Christ. Before Christ you read and see of His coming. Afterwards, you see new teachings, modeling pathways and instructions how to live after His departure.

Has He Come and Departed? Yes. The responsibility is to live accordingly to His teaching and instruction preparing for His return through the eyes of Paul inspired teachings. Concerning the day of His return; no one knows, not even the angels Matthew 24:36. Therefore you must be ready because He is coming Matthew 24:44. How will He come? He will come like a thief 2 Peter 3:10 with clouds and every eye will see Him Revelation 1:7. For the Lord will descend from heaven with voice commands, with a voice of archangel and with trumpets of God 1Thessanian 4:16-17.

The question at hand, will you live the life He has predestined for you according to Jeremiah 29:11. For God know the plan He has for you, plans to prosper, and not ham you, plans to give you hope and a future.

Belove, let not your heart be troubled or fear His plan for your life. Regardless to weather we have done all things well or not. Start today, right now. First, acknowledge you need a Savior, accept Jesus as Lord, believe on Jesus, began the work of renewing your mind to align your life with God's word. Assuredly, there is nobody like Jesus!

Living after the Death of Jesus and the death of your old unrenewed sinful nature is living your best life. Thank you, Jesus!

The song by Johnathan McReynolds comes to mind called *"Got to Have You"*. *The lyrics go something like this:*

> *I got to have you.*
>
> *I got to have you.*
>
> *I got to have you.*
>
> *I got to have you.*
>
> *Oh Lord! I got to have you.*

Your love is guarantee in a world of changes. You turn my world inside out. I am loving what you are all about. If you take your love from me, I do not know what I will do. There is a giant whole in my heart that only you can fill. I got to have you!

I hope I am not too late. I want you Lord, everything else is insignificant. I want you Lord!

God Speaks:

> *Come home my parodical child. I have been waiting for this moment to be restored again. With*

my arms open wide reaching to draw you near and while all of heaven rejoice for you. COME! I love you my child! Your past is not important. What is important is this very moment you decided to come. My soul shouts with joy, I love you and no, it is not too late. Selah.

CPSIA information can be obtained
at www.ICGtesting.com
Printed in the USA
LVHW090225130321
681074LV00005B/218